Workbook

Workbook

**Mike Sprenger
and Kevin Higham**

MONARCH
BOOKS

Oxford, UK & Grand Rapids, Michigan, USA

First published in the UK in 2006 by Monarch Books
(a publishing imprint of Lion Hudson plc),
Mayfield House, 256 Banbury Road, Oxford OX2 7DH
Tel: +44 (0) 1865 302750   Fax: +44 (0) 1865 302757
Email: monarch@lionhudson.com
www.lionhudson.com

ISBN-13: 978-1-85424-777-3 (UK)
ISBN-10: 1-85424-777-8 (UK)
ISBN-13: 978-0-8254-6140-8 (USA)
ISBN-10: 0-8254-6140-5 (USA)

Distributed by:
UK: Marston Book Services Ltd, PO Box 269,
Abingdon, Oxon OX14 4YN;
USA: Kregel Publications, PO Box 2607,
Grand Rapids, Michigan 49501.

British Library Cataloguing Data
A catalogue record for this book is available from the British Library.

Printed and bound in Malta by Gutenberg Press.

Contents

the power of
one

One child supported by one sponsor through Compassion is a powerful and enduring way to tackle world poverty. Compassion seeks out some of the world's most vulnerable children and through individual sponsors provides them with the means to break the cycle of poverty and create a viable future. Working exclusively through local churches in developing countries, Compassion ensures that there is financial integrity, long term commitment and the opportunity for every child to hear and respond to the good news of Jesus Christ.

Become part of Compassion's unique Christ centred, child focused and church based ministry today by contacting your nearest Compassion office:

UK: www.compassionuk.org, 01932 836490

US: www.compassion.com, (800) 336 7676

Australia: www.compassion.com.au, 1 800 224 453

Canada: www.compassion.ca, 1 800 563 5437

New Zealand: www.tearfund.org.nz, 0800 800 777

Compassion UK, 43 High Street, Weybridge, Surrey KT13 8BB

Registered Charity Number 1077216

TRANSFORM A CHILD IN JESUS' NAME AND YOU BEGIN TO CHANGE THE WORLD

Foreword
Unconditional Love

As statistics on church membership decrease in the United Kingdom and throughout Europe, Christians face a crucial challenge. The challenge is firstly to motivate and equip the body of Christ to present the gospel to a needy world. And secondly, to ask the question, "Do the people we are trying to reach understand what we are trying to tell them?" Blowing Your Cover addresses both these crucial aspects as it equips the believer with practical, down-to-earth tools as well as asking the important question, "Are we connecting with the people we are so desperate to reach?"

In the last two years, I have had an encounter with God that has helped shape my perception of evangelism. John 3:16 expresses this very clearly. "For God so loved the world that he gave his one and only Son…" It was love that motivated God into action. So what is evangelism? It starts when we have love in our hearts for the people around us and this love motivates us to step out into all sorts of responses and actions. Here is something profound and relevant for the post-modern mindset of today. In our sceptical, cynical world how will people know that the message of Jesus Christ is true? Answer, when they meet real love. For when they see our love and experience it, there will be openness to our words.

Let me encourage you with a metaphor: "Be a pastor to those around you." Love people unconditionally and always seek their spiritual welfare. The challenge for each of us is to ask God the specific question, "Who am I called to love?"

In 1 Corinthians, the apostle Paul talks of many things. He talks of faith, hope and love, but the greatest of these is love. I am convinced that Blowing Your Cover will equip you practically to express this love to the world around you.

Laurence Singlehurst
April 2006

Introduction

Welcome to your Blowing Your Cover Workbook. This Workbook consists of six sessions that will empower and release you into your lifestyle of evangelism.

Most Christians would like to be able to share their faith more confidently and effectively; you are obviously one of them – that's why you are holding this Workbook in your hands. We are convinced that the training you are going to receive in lifestyle evangelism, covering the six sessions in this Workbook and beyond, will equip you to be more effective in communicating the gospel of Jesus to those around you.

Remember, God wants to use you! Don't look to other people to do the work for you. You can contribute hope, you can be influential and you can make a difference to your family, friends, associates and anyone else that God brings into your life.

The purpose of this course is clear: to help you to be more effective in sharing the life-changing message of the gospel, the very same message that has made such a difference to your own life.

You are about to embark on an exciting journey, a journey that thousands of people around the country have already completed, many with life-changing results. Our prayer is that, as you share your faith, you will have the joy of seeing some of your friends saved and added to your local church.

Enjoy the journey!

Mike Sprenger
Kevin Higham

Session 1

Communicating the Gospel

Welcome to Blowing Your Cover. Over the next few weeks we will be focusing on releasing you into your lifestyle of evangelism; so sit back, relax and enjoy the journey. We want to put the word "fun" alongside the word "evangelism" and watch what God will do. Throughout the course and beyond, many opportunities to share your faith will come your way, so it is vital that you are able to communicate effectively the important aspects of the Christian message. You also need to be able to lead someone to faith should the opportunity arise.

Below are the aims of the first session.

1. To understand the importance of the gospel
2. To be able to communicate the gospel visually
3. To be able to discern when a person is ready to become a Christian
4. To be able to lead that person to Jesus
5. To be sure of that person's conversion

Let us start by reminding ourselves of the main points of the gospel message.

The gospel

Mark 8:34–36

Then he called the crowd to him along with his disciples and said: "If anyone would come after me, he must deny himself and take up his cross and follow me. For whoever wants to save his life will lose it, but whoever loses his life for me and for the *gospel* will save it. What good is it for a man to gain the whole world, yet forfeit his soul?" (emphasis added)

The gospel – so what is it?

Romans 1:1–5 tells us:
- It's God's gospel.
- It's not something new.
- It's all about Jesus.
- It's intended for all.

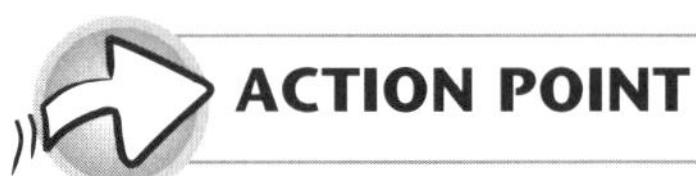

ACTION POINT

Place all the relevant verses in the correct box.

After completing your given set of Bible verses below, spend a few moments considering the implications for your non-Christian friends and for yourself.

God is...   1 Peter 1:16; 1 John 1:9; 1 John 4:16

Loving

Holy

Faithful and just

Our Friends...　　Romans 3:22–24; Romans 6:23; Isaiah 53:6

Have turned their backs on God and do not accept what God has done

Deserve an eternity without God but there is hope for them in the gospel

Could have eternal life

Jesus...　　Romans 5:8; Ephesians 2:8–9; John 1:1, 14

Is God, who became man

Died for our friends

Offers our friends salvation as a free gift

The Decision...　　1 John 1:8–9; 1 Peter 3:15; Isaiah 64:6

Even good works are not enough

Our friends must ask Jesus to forgive their sins

Our friends must ask Jesus to be Lord of their lives

The Result...   2 Corinthians 5:17; Acts 1:8 and Jeremiah 29:11;
2 Corinthians 5:18

Reconciliation with God

A new life in Christ

A life empowered and
given destiny by God

Implications... ?

The Great Commission

> **Matthew 28:18–20**
>
> Then Jesus came to them and said, "All authority in heaven and on earth has been given to me. Therefore **go** and make disciples of all nations, baptising them in the name of the Father and of the Son and of the Holy Spirit, and teaching them to obey everything I have commanded you. And surely I am with you always, to the very end of the age."
>
> (emphasis added)

Let's focus on the word "**go**".

"**Go**" is a powerful word. The dictionary defines "**go**" as "the quality of being full of activity". So we need to make sure our lives are full of the right type of activity, the type that produces the most fruit.

Before Jesus ascended into heaven his final command to his disciples was to "**go**". This command powerfully propelled them into action that made an amazing impact on the world of their day. The literal translation of this word means, "As you are going", and was spoken when referring to people's daily lives. Effectively Jesus was saying, "As you are going about your daily life, make disciples."

We too are called to **go** and do the same.

Why go?

- Out of love for others – 2 Corinthians 5:14
- Out of a passion for the truth – John 8:32
- Out of concern for the world – 1 Thessalonians 5:1–3
- Out of a desire to see God glorified – 2 Thessalonians 1:11–12

Write down the role your church plays in evangelism.

Write down the role that you play in evangelism.

In the adjacent box, draw four circles that represent the rough percentage of your week involved in:

- Family life
- Work
- Social activities
- Evangelism

Presenting the gospel

As you meet with, and pray for, those in your sphere of influence, opportunities will arise in which you will be able to communicate the gospel. The following is a visual method of sharing this good news with others, which can be easily memorised.

1. Begin by drawing a big letter "C" with two ellipses at the top and bottom. In the top one, write the word "God". List some of his characteristics as shown, e.g. holy, eternal, then end with the fact that he is the creator. Now write the word "People" in the bottom ellipse, explaining that God and humankind enjoyed a relationship with each other.

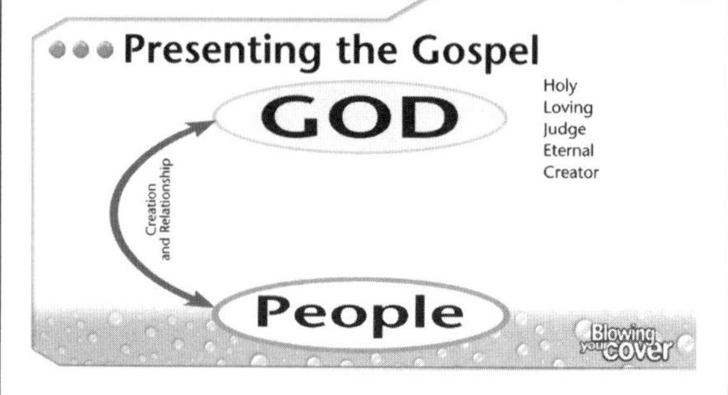

Lastly, turn the remaining arc into a double-headed arrow and write "Creation & Relationship" along it.

2. Draw a cross over the double-headed arrows and explain that when humankind disobeyed God, sin entered the world, putting a barrier between them. Draw the cloud and list some of the results of sin, e.g being dead to God, physical death and humanity's sinful nature.

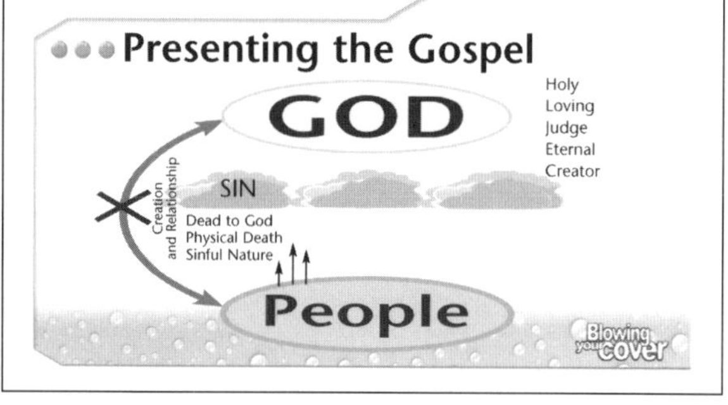

Now draw in the little arrows, which reach up from "People" to "God". Explain that humans try to find purpose and fulfilment in life through relationships, status or even religion. However, no matter how hard they try, they cannot reach God. Shade in the bottom ellipse to highlight how totally sinful and corrupt humanity is before God.

3. Draw a large arrow from "God" to "People". Explain that God out of his great mercy and love sent his son Jesus into the world.

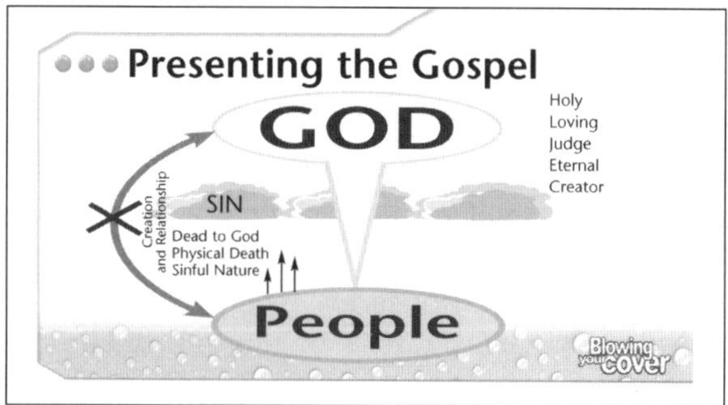

4. Jesus lived an amazing life but came primarily to die in our place. Draw in the cross and explain what happened when Jesus died, using these verses: "…without the shedding of blood there is no forgiveness" (Hebrews 9:22) and "Jesus answered, 'I am the way and the truth and the life. No one comes to the Father except through me.'" (John 14:6).

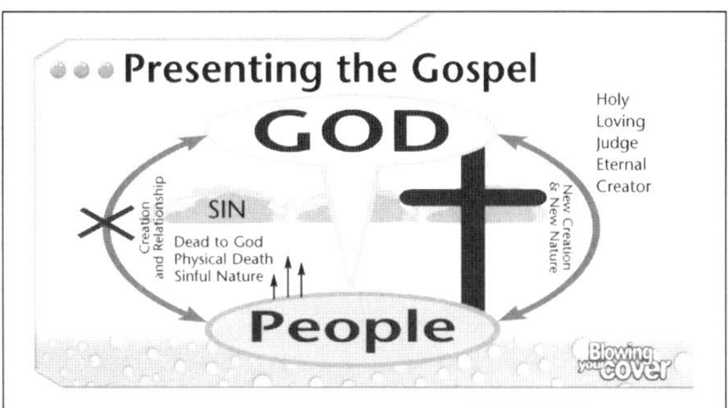

Explain in more detail the implications of the cross, specifically how God's judgement was satisfied. Finally, complete the last part of the missing circle, writing "New Creation & New Nature" along the arrow. Talk about what it means to be a new creation in Christ, reconciled to God, and to have received a new nature.

Taking that vital step

Sometimes as we share the gospel, some people will be ready to respond and make a decision to become a Christian. The following are helpful pointers for you to assess where people stand, and ultimately lead those who are ready into a living faith and a firm commitment to Christ.

Work together with the Holy Spirit

The Holy Spirit has already been working in the life of the person concerned; therefore, we need to co-operate with the Holy Spirit – like a midwife in helping a birth. We can't start or stop it. If they are ready to become a Christian explain that this will be the most exciting step they will ever make. As they take this step the Holy Spirit may also touch delicate issues in their lives – not because he's unjust but because he wants the best for them. Therefore remember to be sensitive.

During the conversation check that they:

- Believe that Jesus is the Son of God
- Believe that Jesus died on the cross for their sin

- Have come to the point of wanting to become a Christian
- Are ready to let God have Lordship over their lives
- Are ready to accept God's forgiveness

If not, they may still be in the process of thinking the issues through.

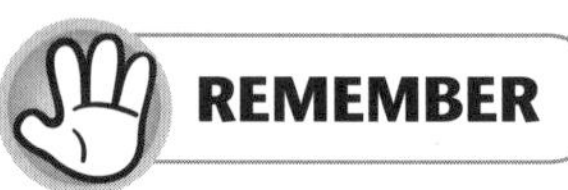

REMEMBER

Each individual needs to be ready to make their own decision in their own time.

Pray

Pray together and lead them in a prayer if they are unsure what to say.

- Help them to ask for God's forgiveness.
- Help them to ask for God's leadership from now on in their life.
- Help them to ask for God's power to live a Spirit-filled life.

After praying remember:

- Not everyone will react the same way. Some people may become emotional and others may not react at all. What matters is that they took a step of faith, not that some specific feeling is evoked.
- An excellent verse to reinforce their decision is Luke 15:10, "… there is rejoicing in the presence of the angels of God over one sinner who repents."

What next?

- Stick with your friend and be prepared to disciple them.
- Go to church meetings and worship God together.
- Help your friend develop Christian friendships, including becoming involved in Alpha, similar enquirer courses or a small group.
- Encourage your friend to pray and read the Bible regularly.
- Encourage your friend to be baptised.
- Encourage your friend to maintain their existing friendships where possible.
- Teach them who they are in Christ.

All these changes will not happen at once so don't overwhelm your friend. They are produced by the work of the Holy Spirit and it is not for us to try to force people into a certain mould.

Follow through

REMEMBER

Genuine conversions result in:

- Peace with God
- An authentic love for God
- A desire to meet with other Christians
- A desire to pray
- A teachable nature
- An awareness of the presence of God

These may not happen at once.

IMPORTANT

Commit yourself to making sure you or someone else looks after these new Christians. Discipleship is vital, as we need to give these new Christians a firm foundation on which to build their new lives.

Situation One

Jim works in your office and you have been praying for him for three months. This is the third time you have had lunch together. At lunch you ask Jim if you can briefly explain what it means to be a Christian. Jim is extremely interested in the gospel and ready to become a Christian.

What do you say or do?

Situation Two

Two of you are visiting Jane, a single mother whose son attends the "Kidz Club" that your church runs. You visit her house every week to call on her son. Two months ago in response to her ill health, you had the opportunity to pray for physical healing. On arriving she pours out her heart to you. She says she is not able to cope with life and asks for help.

What do you say or do?

Key Scripture

KEY SCRIPTURE

Romans 3:23–24

"...for all have sinned and fall short of the glory of God,
and are justified freely by his grace..."

Session 2

Your Sphere of Influence

Welcome

Welcome to Session Two of Blowing Your Cover. The aims for this session are covered below.

1. To start your Friendship List by prayerfully selecting people from your sphere of influence
2. To know your two strongest evangelism styles
3. To recognise the evangelism styles of people in your group

Key Scripture from Session One

Understanding your friends

In each of the circles write the name of a friend that you are in regular contact with and would love to see become a Christian.

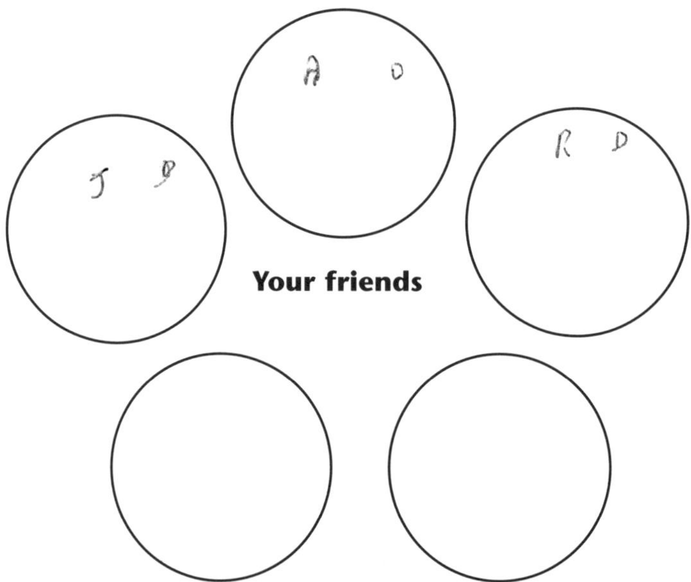

Meet a typical friend:

- They may have rejected the idea of going to church, but they have not rejected the idea of God.
- Even though they have few absolute morals, they secretly want them for themselves and for their children if they have any.
- If questioned they do not really know what they believe.
- They may actually try going to church if someone asks them.
- They will ditch your friendship if they think they are your project and not your friend.
- They want to know and experience something.
- They are probably more willing to talk about God than you think and may well want you to start a conversation.

As your friends receive answers to some of their questions, they move closer to being more interested in Jesus and Christianity.

Moving our friends along

"Disbeliever" to "New Believer" scale

Your friends' interest in Christianity tends to fall into one of the following categories:

- Disbeliever
- Doubter
- Observer
- Seeker

IMPORTANT

Evangelism is a process – it involves moving a person from their location on the scale to becoming a New Believer. (We are not labelling people here, rather helping ourselves to understand where our friends might be on their journey.)

Scale	Disbeliever	Doubter
Description	They do not believe in a supreme being and are cynical about Christianity.	They are not sure Christianity is true. They are sceptical about it.
Hints & Tips	Live a Christian life in front of these people.	Tell them how real Jesus is to you.

Scale	Observer	Seeker
Description	They do not see an immediate need to believe in Christ, but are willing to examine any claims that are made.	They are willing to talk about the relevance of the gospel.
Hints & Tips	Ask them questions concerning eternal issues and provide them with relevant reading materials.	Take the initiative to share the gospel or invite them to an Alpha or similar enquirer's course.

Scale	New Believer
Description	They display the fruits of repentance and faith. They are new disciples, willing to be integrated into the church and continuing to grow in character, lifestyle and service.
IMPORTANT	Someone needs to support and disciple them.

Which of the four types (Disbeliever, Doubter, Observer or Seeker) do you think best describes your five friends that you listed in the circles?

	Name	Type
1.		
2.		
3.		
4.		
5.		

Introducing the Friendship List

From the five people above, write down in the space below the names of two friends you would like to see become Christians:

MY FRIENDSHIP LIST
Name One

Name Two

The way it will work:

- **Your Friendship List** – two people you meet with and pray for on a regular basis.
- **Your small-group's Friendship List** – the combined number of names from everyone in the small-group. The group is encouraged to pray for these people on a regular basis.

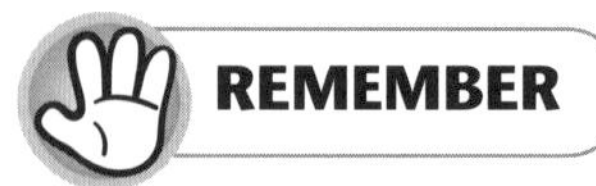

Friendships can be difficult to maintain at times. However, we need to show the love of God and develop friendships that last, regardless of whether or not people agree with the Christian message.

DISCUSSION

■ Situation One

You are with a non-Christian friend walking in the country; all around you there is beauty, spectacular scenery and the wonders of creation…

What do you say or do?

■ Situation Two

Your non-Christian friend switches on the CD player in your car and worship music starts playing…

What do you say or do?

> **Divine appointments**
> "I don't expect you to tell everyone you meet day in and day out that you are a Christian but I do expect you to say something when God obviously opens the door."
> (Steve Hill, evangelist)

■ **Situation Three**

Stitched up by God

You're on a training course with other people from your company. The consultant would like you to introduce yourself to the group by filling in a large piece of paper with the following information and allow them to ask questions about your answers.

1. A country you would like to visit.
2. Someone you would like to spend 24 hours with.
3. A phrase that someone would say about you.

As you watch the DVD think through what you would have said or done. Remember sometimes the obvious is not the best answer!

Sharing Your Faith

What must it be?

- Natural
- Personal

How is it achieved?

- Verbally
- Gradually
- Through being empowered by the Holy Spirit.

What effect does this have on you?

- We should be "salt and light"
- We should become "living letters"

We are all different! You do not have to be a famous evangelist; God wants to use you. Remember, he wants you to be yourself.

YOU ARE UNIQUE!

Blowing Your Cover questionnaire

DIRECTIONS

On a scale of 0 to 3 record your response to each of the following 40 statements:

0 Not at all
1 Rarely
2 Often
3 Always

_____ 1. I can persuade others to help me in achieving my objectives.

_____ 2. I am quiet and unassuming.

_____ 3. I prefer to follow guidelines rather than develop my own way.

_____ 4. I am quick to act without thinking about the consequences.

_____ 5. I naturally gather other people to me.

_____ 6. My friends say that I am a good listener.

_____ 7. I prefer to talk to people face to face than speak to them on the telephone.

_____ 8. When presented with a new opportunity I feel confident to tackle it.

_____ 9. I like to think matters through logically.

_____ 10. I am a disciplined person.

_____ 11. I am a friendly person.

_____ 12. I am accused of being private and stubborn at times.

_____ 13. I enjoy winning people over to my point of view.

_____ 14. I seek both support and feedback from others before making important decisions.

_____ 15. I give my time and abilities generously to others.

_____ 16. I can be very talkative.

_____ 17. I am someone who does not wear their heart on their sleeve.

_____ 18. I find it difficult to be direct with someone.

_____ 19. Confronting people comes easily to me.

_____ 20. It is important to me to have goals to achieve.

_____ 21. I am described as unemotional.

_____ 22. I will take the initiative in a situation.

_____ 23. I believe that actions speak louder than words.

_____ 24. I love talking to people about my dreams, visions and aspirations.

_____ 25. I take the safer option when given a choice.

_____ 26. I am able to act quickly when the need arises.

_____ 27. I enjoy coaching and counselling people.

_____ 28. Once I have made a decision I will remain steadfast in purpose until a more logical alternative comes along.

_____ 29. I love taking risks.

_____ 30. Any advice I give is based on thorough understanding of the circumstances.

_____ 31. I help people practically rather than communicate my beliefs through words.

_____ 32. It is important to me that people hear the truth of the gospel.

_____ 33. Achieving results is important to me.

_____ 34. I am a popular person.

_____ 35. In discussions I am able to help people identify the central issues.

_____ 36. In conversation I get straight to the point and avoid small talk.

_____ 37. I see problems as challenges.

_____ 38. When I know that someone else is in need I naturally want to respond to them.

_____ 39. I prefer to be with other people than on my own.

_____ 40. I am told I need to be more gentle and compassionate when dealing with others.

Transfer your answers to the table below, total each column, and then record the two highest scores.

Total table

Type	Direct	Personal	Thinker	Helper
	4	1	3	2
	12	5	9	6
	19	8	10	7
	22	11	17	14
	26	13	21	15
	29	16	25	18
	33	20	28	23
	36	24	30	27
	37	34	32	31
	40	39	35	38
Total:				

From the table, what style(s) best describes you?

Styles:

1.

2.

DIRECT

Some traits that best describe this style are as follows:

These people tend to be businesslike when relating to others. They are predominately assertive, quick to act, results-orientated and opportunistic. They like to make things happen and enjoy both challenges and taking risks.

Likely strengths are:

- Natural leaders
- Highly motivated
- Focused
- Risk takers

Possible areas for development:

- Empathy for others
- Patience
- Flexibility
- Being willing to compromise
- Can overwhelm the hearer, help is needed from others with different styles

Evangelistic opportunities

- Good at taking the opportunity to question people about their faith
- Able to express their faith with passion and expectancy

PERSONAL

Some traits that best describe this style are as follows:

These people tend to be friendly, emotional, inspiring and are comfortable in social environments. They can freely engage in small talk before engaging in the task at hand. They are feeling-orientated, can be visionaries, while enjoying applause and recognition.

Likely strengths are:

- Responsive and friendly
- Motivators
- Fun to be around
- Enthusiastic
- Creative

Possible areas for development:

- Pay more attention to detail
- Watch emotional control
- Need to prioritise
- Learn their limits
- Learn to set goals

Evangelistic opportunities

- Good at recognising friends in public places and greeting them
- Often have divine appointments with new people who come into their sphere of influence

THINKER

Some traits that best describe this style are as follows:

These people tend to be deliberate, cautious, constrained and logical. They remain steadfast in purpose and are often more concerned with what people think rather than what they feel. They can often be slow to make deep friendships.

Likely strengths are:

- Problem solvers
- Extremely practical
- They perform jobs well
- Good at planning
- Steady and reliable

Possible areas for development:

- Develop relational skills
- Actively plan to spend more time with others
- Make a conscious effort not to interrupt others
- Need to take other people's opinions on board
- Need to be more willing to take risks

Evangelistic opportunities

- Spend time thinking through how to apply the Christian message to what is going on in the world today
- Because they are natural strategists, their actions may well have a great impact on others

HELPER

Some traits that best describe this style are as follows:

These people tend to be quiet, unassuming and supportive. They are warm and friendly listeners who work well with others. They enjoy personal contact and shared responsibility. They prefer to avoid confrontations where possible.

Likely strengths are:

- Good listeners and advisors
- Dedicated
- Trustworthy
- They show love through actions rather than words
- Attach value to menial tasks

Possible areas for development:

- Become more independent
- Learn to set deadlines/tasks/targets
- Learn to express their point of view confidently
- May need to be more assertive at times
- Learn to say "No" sometimes

Evangelistic opportunities

- Are always serving people in their sphere of influence
- Often have the platform to speak up because they have already won the respect of others

Make a note of the styles of the other members in your small-group.

Who in your small-group has a style that would get on well with those on your Friendship List?

IMPORTANT

Knowing your style will help you and your small-group to be more effective in sharing your faith with others.

Key Scripture

KEY SCRIPTURE

Romans 6:23
"For the wages of sin is death, but the gift of God
is eternal life in Christ Jesus our Lord."

Session 3

Connecting with Your Culture

Welcome

Welcome to Session Three of Blowing Your Cover. The aims for this session are covered below.

AIMS

> 1. To gain an understanding of our culture
> 2. To add a third person to your Friendship List
> 3. To examine culture connecting qualities

Key Scripture from Session Two

Understanding our culture

Cultures are different across the world. These differences can occur both within a country and in a local area; therefore, understanding our target culture(s) is essential. For instance, in the UK we have moved from modern culture to post-modern culture.

In our desire to reach the people on our Friendship List we need to understand their background/culture.

Reaching someone with a Christian background is different from reaching a person from a secular background or people from a different ethnic group. The apostle Paul used a different initial approach in Athens from the one he used in Jerusalem. Whatever culture we are living in or trying to reach, the universal key, as Paul shows, is to build relationships. Over time and through friendship, we can demonstrate and communicate the gospel. As we spend time with people we gradually and continually expose them to the gospel. This "drip, drip" approach can leave our friends thirsty for more and should not alienate them.

For a more detailed look at Western culture please examine the additional reading material at the end of this workbook.

As we engage in evangelism, we should never become "salesmen" for the gospel, simply transmitting data to those who "buy" our product. Instead, we must realise that the gospel involves loving people and building relationships.

If our view of evangelism is simply to get others to agree that four or five thoughts about Christianity are correct, pray a prayer, and then go to heaven when they die; then we are missing a vital element. We are called to make disciples; therefore, our task is to bring those on our Friendship List into a twofold relationship. The first relationship is that of coming to know God personally, living for him and enjoying him both now and for ever. The second is to help people become rooted into the house of God, where they can grow in their newfound faith.

Winning others to Christ and making disciples is all about connecting with our culture and building these all-important relationships.

Below is a picture of a typical evangelist.

Is this your perception of the best way to communicate the gospel? Are we all meant to be evangelists?

What is the difference between an evangelist and someone who shares their faith on a regular basis? See Acts 8:4–8.

Take a break

Looking with the eyes of faith

In your mind's eye think about the people on your Friendship List.

Start to think about one or two of these people giving their lives to Christ! Take a couple of minutes right now to picture this in your mind. Picture their reaction and responses. Now think about your response on hearing that they have become Christians.

It's easy to look at evangelism as being something that only trained specialists get involved in, or to feel that evangelism only happens when a few enthusiasts take to the streets to talk to strangers. There is a need for full-time evangelists and street outreach, but networking is something that EVERYONE can be involved in. Blowing Your Cover calls this "your sphere of influence".

Adding a third name to your Friendship List

Everybody has people they meet regularly, namely **family**, **friends**, **neighbours** (people living nearby) and **associates** (at work, or an educational institution, for example). You don't have to start up "cold" conversations with these people, because the foundations of relationships have already been laid.

Friendships will demand patience, creativity, most probably being a "servant" and a definite commitment to the long haul. As we build relationships and show love to the people God brings into our lives, then Disbelievers, Doubters and Observers can become Seekers. In time, we will also have the joy of seeing some of them being saved and added into God's family. God wants to use you to connect with your culture and to see people who are on your Friendship List added to his Church.

> **Acts 2:47**
> **"And the Lord added to their number daily those**
> **who were being saved."**

Your sphere of influence

Who are the people in your sphere of influence? Write their names below and tick the relevant box.

FAMILY, FRIENDS, NEIGHBOURS and ASSOCIATES

Name	Disbeliever	Doubter	Observer	Seeker
	❑	❑	❑	❑
	❑	❑	❑	❑
	❑	❑	❑	❑
	❑	❑	❑	❑

> **"You can make more friends in two months by being**
> **interested in other people than you can in two years by**
> **trying to get people interested in you."**
> **(Dale Carnegie, *How to Win Friends and Influence People*)**

Prayerfully select one of the above people and add them to your Friendship List from Session Two. The three names now on your list are:

<table>
<tr><th colspan="1" align="center">MY FRIENDSHIP LIST</th></tr>
<tr><td>Name One</td></tr>
<tr><td>Name Two</td></tr>
<tr><td>Name Three</td></tr>
</table>

Culture-connecting qualities

Remember the friends we talked about in Session Two – our desire is for some of them to become Christians and to be introduced to God's family: the Church. Yet these friends are immersed within the current culture. In order to reach them with the gospel message it is helpful to think about six culture-connecting qualities that as Christians we need to develop and display.

1. Compassion not duty

This is where it all starts. God's compassion is revealed to us through the life, death and resurrection of Christ. We see the same compassion demonstrated within the life of Christ; for instance, we read in Mark 1:41, "Filled with compassion, Jesus reached out his hand and touched the man." As we are disciples of Christ we too should desire this compassion.

The very nature of compassion is all about being, not just doing. Quite often out of duty we feel obliged to be there for our friends, when the real response should flow out of unconditional love. Very often we are encouraged to pastor our Christian friends, which is admirable, but we also need to pastor our non-Christian friends as well.

Compassion, then, should flow out of our very innermost being, as an overflow of our life in Christ and our desire to be like him.

2. Friendship not projects

We often hear Christians use certain words in connection with their friends, such as "befriend" and "contact". For example, "He is on my contact list" or "I intend to befriend her to encourage her to come to church!" Whilst their intentions are good, the very nature of the thinking behind these comments conveys a sense of making your friend a project.

Friendships are valuable and we need to grow and develop them with the help of God. A good friendship is based on trust and achieved over a period of time. It is not something that can be rushed. Sometimes we can go out of our way to try and "meet new friends" when actually they are closer than we think.

Some people meet their friends in the workplace; for others it may be the club, school or college. Wherever you meet your friends make sure you take time out to spend with them, enjoy their company and take an interest in them.

3. Active listening not prejudgement

Listening is not the same as hearing. Often people hear but they don't actively listen to what their friends are saying. We need to be people who actively listen to the words of our friends, both spoken and unspoken.

Active listening is a way of listening and responding to your friends that improves understanding. When people talk to each other, they don't always listen attentively. They can easily be distracted, are half listening, or they are thinking about something else. When people are sharing their faith, they are often busy formulating a response to what is being said. They assume that they have heard what their friend is saying, so rather than paying attention, they focus on how they can respond to win the argument.

Remember, we are not sharing our faith to win an argument, but to demonstrate the love of Christ. Sadly, we can end up prejudging people by jumping to a conclusion without first hearing and actively listening to what they are really saying.

4. Conversation not Christian monologue

Conversation by definition is a two-way street and follows on from active listening. It involves taking the time to ask your friends open questions – questions that will open up the conversation further to allow you to explore more about their lives and for them to ask more about your life.

However, as we have just learnt, we need to listen to the answers. After a conversation has been started it is important to be aware of the direction the conversation is taking and how the other person is responding. Based on that assessment, make a decision on whether to continue the conversation or move to a different topic. It is important we do not simply "offload" onto our friends and end up with nothing more than a Christian monologue.

Be prepared, though, to enter into a full-length conversation about Christ when the opportunity arises. However, also be prepared to tell them only part of the story and leave them asking for more! The possibilities are endless and exciting!

Below are some questions designed to open up conversation and encourage active listening:

- Why do you think people prefer to live as if God does not exist?
- How do you teach your children right from wrong?
- If you could have God change one thing in your life, what would it be?
- What are your views regarding life after death?
- In your opinion how does someone become a Christian?
- How are you looking for happiness in this life?
- Does your worldview allow for any absolutes?

IMPORTANT

Bridge of friendship

Before we rush headlong into confronting our non-Christian friends, it is vital that we consider how strong our friendship is. If the trust level is insufficient, then our endeavours could permanently hinder our friendship.

In the first picture you see the basic state of affairs. In this situation there exists a bridge of friendship that will support a maximum load of ten tonnes.

In the second picture what this Christian is trying to accomplish, in one encounter, is to drive the whole gospel over the bridge of friendship. In this illustration a 40-tonne lorry represents this attempt.

Of course, it does not take a genius to know that this approach is doomed to fail, as the bridge will collapse under the weight. In some cases the bridge of friendship is permanently broken as the non-Christian thinks you are just out to "Bible bash" them.

This can be easily avoided. Instead of trying to communicate the whole gospel at one sitting, you can break it down into smaller and more manageable portions that will not cause the bridge of friendship to collapse. In reality this means praying and working away over a period of time in order to strengthen the bridge of friendship, so it can support heavier loads. Remember, we can gauge how strong the bridge is by observing people's reactions. Listen out for the telltale sounds of the bridge of friendship creaking under the strain.

As we spend time with our friends, showing love and genuine concern, this should create a foundation stone where trust and respect can flourish. Arising out of this will come many opportunities to share your faith. Some Christians miss this and their friendship ends in disaster.

If you continue to be patient, bold and wise you will eventually have the opportunity to communicate the whole gospel with many of your friends. The bridge of friendship remains intact, possibly even stronger than it was at first.

5. Conviction not condemnation

Our friends are on a spiritual journey and as we keep walking with them we are able to demonstrate the love and truths of God through our lives. Be confident that the Holy Spirit will start to convict some of them just as he did with you. Remember it is his job to convict, not ours. We should not condemn our friends but allow them to come to Christ in their way and in their time.

Matthew 7:1–2 says, "Do not judge, or you too will be judged. For in the same way as you judge others, you will be judged, and with the measure you use, it will be measured to you."

As your friendship grows, you will have many opportunities to share the gospel. Therefore, continue to pray that the Holy Spirit will convict your friends of their spiritual condition.

6. Conversion and new life

As God works in the lives of the friends on your Friendship List, you will have the opportunity of leading some of them to Christ. Let's look at three examples of conversion.

Look at Luke 19:1–10. What do we learn about how Zacchaeus was converted?

Look at Acts 16:13–15. What do we learn about how Lydia was converted?

Look at Acts 2:37–46. What do we learn about the changes that took place in the people of Jerusalem?

ACTION POINT

How would you evaluate where you are in terms of how you are relating to your friends on your Friendship List? Are there areas that need strengthening or is there a specific action that you need to take and pray about?

Use the table below to write down the names of your friends and then how well you excel in the culture-connecting qualities. Think through an action plan to help you take the next step with your friends.

	Name	Where you are now?	Action plan
1.			
2.			
3.			

Key Scripture

KEY SCRIPTURE

Romans 5:8
"But God demonstrates his own love for us in this:
While we were still sinners, Christ died for us."

Session 4

The Impact of Your Life

Welcome to Session Four of Blowing Your Cover. The aims for this session are covered below.

1. To understand how your life influences others
2. To write down your personal story
3. To start work on your personal tract

Key Scripture from Session Three

Lifestyle evangelism

In the space provided, please write as many common ways of presenting the gospel as you can think of, e.g. in the open air.

Open air	

When we consider the most common ways of presenting the gospel we need to ask the question, "How effective are these methods?"

In a poll of 10,000 people who were asked the question, "What made you first come to church?", the following results were obtained:

1%	Were contacted through specific outreach
3%	Just walked in
7%	Came because of a special need
8%	Were attracted by the presence of the church and the pastor's ministry
81%	Were invited by relatives and friends

The table above clearly illustrates how important it is for you to develop friendships with those who don't know Jesus. One way that your life can make an impact on these people is through the power of your own story – both in spoken and written form.

Learning how to write your story

Spoken and written stories have always played an important part in church history. The apostle Paul on several occasions told his personal story of how Jesus had met with him. The very word "witness" means someone who speaks about things that they have seen, heard and experienced.

Paul developed the practise of telling the story of how he became a Christian and he used it to great effect.

Read Acts 26:12–29 and make a note of the main points of his story.

Writing your story

- It is one of the most powerful and important weapons you have.
- It's a truthful account of how you became a Christian and therefore it is difficult to argue against.

 **IMPORTANT**

Let's think – process or event?

When thinking about your story consider the following questions:

Before Conversion (B.C.)

- What was your purpose in life?
- How did you deal with feelings of guilt?
- What was your attitude towards God?
- How did you expect to get to heaven?
- What did you believe about Jesus Christ?
- By what influences and/or experiences did God bring you to faith in Jesus?

During Conversion (D.C.)

- What convinced you that Jesus is God's Son?
- How did he convict you of your sinfulness?
- What led you to rely on Jesus rather than on yourself for a right relationship with God?
- When did you pray to receive Jesus as Saviour and Lord?
- What did you say to God?

After Conversion (A.C.)

- Who is Jesus and how is he your Saviour?
- What does it mean to have him as Lord of your life?
- How is life different since you received Christ?
- What changes have there been in how you live and what you live for?
- What is your relationship with God like?

IMPORTANT

Do not focus on the sin; instead focus on Christ.

1. In the years leading up to becoming a Christian, describe where you were spiritually.

2. What caused you to begin considering God/Jesus?

3. What made you finally realise that you needed to become a Christian?

4. How did you receive Jesus?

5. How has Jesus changed your life?

If you became a Christian when you were a child then focus upon questions 4 and 5.

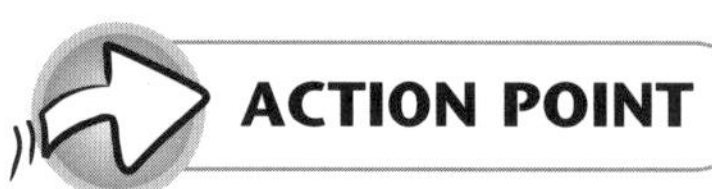

Practise telling your story

At this point your trainer will ask for one volunteer to tell their story to the whole group.

Your personal tract

Opportunities/divine appointments will come your way to make friends with people you have never met before. When this occurs, have you ever wished that you had something relevant to give to someone to read, after you have talked with him or her? Do you wish there was a way you could share something about Jesus with people you only see for a few brief minutes, as well as for close friends that you spend a lot of time with?

Personal tracts – short printed accounts of how you came to know God – can be extremely useful tools for such occasions.

NOTES FROM THE PRESENTATION

Mark 4:26–29

- Kingdom of God – like seed

Personal tracts: the why and how

- Useful tool
- They make an impact on the people we meet
- Not rejected because it is your own story
- Lots of opportunities
- Makes a difference

Getting started

- Your story counts
- Select or choose one of the following:
  1. Clear-cut conversion
  2. Healing or provision
  3. Childhood conversion
  4. Gospel presentation

Writing your tract

- Start simply
- Avoid jargon
- Be honest – don't exaggerate
- Use an easy and talkative style
- Avoid long words and too much detail
- Bring Jesus forward

Layout

- Use approximately 450 words
- Choose a good title
- Use headings
- End with church details, i.e. address, telephone number, email etc.
- No personal details
- Talk to your leader about how to print your personal tract

AN EXAMPLE OF THE CONTENT OF
A PERSONAL TRACT

It all started when I was 15 years old. Someone caught my eye: she was tall, with long blonde hair, and I took quite a fancy to her. She invited me to attend the same youth group that she went to. It was from that point on that my life started to change in ways that I could never have imagined. The youth group she invited me to was a church youth group! I'd never really attended church before so I thought it would be boring but, after some weeks, I grew to like the new friends that I had made. I realised that they were normal people like me!

Anyway, it was one Saturday night when a friend asked if he could come to my house to talk about God. He opened his Bible and showed me some words that explained how I was separated from God because of the sin in my life. I couldn't believe what I was hearing – I'd not thought of myself as a sinner before, but he was right, I was separated from God and I knew it! I didn't understand what was happening but tears started to roll down my face. I wanted to say sorry to God for the things I'd done wrong. My friend also showed me from the Bible that Christ died on the cross to bridge the gap between God and me. He showed me that all I needed to do was to pray, confess my sin to God and ask Christ to be the boss of my life. He showed me, again from the Bible, that by doing this I would receive forgiveness from God and that the gap between God and me would be bridged and I would have eternal life! It all sounded too simple but I prayed to God and experienced his forgiveness that night.

I used to think that going to church made you a Christian but how wrong I was – that night I found out that being a Christian involves knowing God personally.

Since that Saturday I have enjoyed getting to know God better. I experience his presence in my life daily and, even though I still get things wrong, he loves and forgives me. I couldn't imagine my life without God. I've discovered that Christianity is far from boring, like I thought it was all those years ago.

If you'd like to know more about becoming a Christian, then why not come along to The Family Church. We meet in Twynham School, Sopers Lane, Christchurch, on a Sunday morning at 10.30 am.

Kevin

A sample tract (not to scale)

Below is an example of a completed personal tract using the previous transcript.

Then I saw her face...

It all started when I was 15 years old. Someone caught my eye: she was tall, with long blonde hair, and I took quite a fancy to her. She invited me to attend the same youth group that she went to. It was from that point on that my life started to change in ways that I could never have imagined. The youth group she invited me to was a church youth group! I'd never really attended church before so I thought it would be boring but, after some weeks, I grew to like the new friends that I had made. I realised that they were normal people like me!

Anyway, it was one Saturday night when a friend asked if he could come to my house to talk about God. He opened his Bible and showed me some words that explained how I was separated from God because of the sin in my life. I couldn't believe what I was hearing – I'd not thought of myself as a sinner before, but he was right, I was separated from God and I knew it! I didn't understand what was happening but tears started to roll down my face. I wanted to say sorry to God for the things I'd done wrong. My friend also showed me from the Bible that Christ died on the cross to bridge the gap between God and me. He showed me that all I needed to do was to pray, confess my sin to God and ask Christ to be the boss of my life. He showed me, again from the Bible, that by doing this I would receive forgiveness from God and that the gap between God and me would be bridged and I would have eternal life! It all sounded too simple but I prayed to God and experienced his forgiveness that night.

I used to think that going to church made you a Christian but how wrong I was – that night I found out that being a Christian involves knowing God personally.

Since that Saturday I have enjoyed getting to know God better. I experience his presence in my life daily and, even though I still get things wrong, he loves and forgives me. I couldn't imagine my life without God. I've discovered that Christianity is far from boring, like I thought it was all those years ago.

If you'd like to know more about becoming a Christian, then why not come along to The Family Church. We meet in Twynham School, Sopers Lane, Christchurch, on a Sunday morning at 10.30 am.

Kevin

Now it's your turn

Now it is time for you to turn your story into a personal tract. Don't be afraid to have a go. You may be pleasantly surprised at the results. Remember, your story has the potential to impact many people's lives.

Using personal tracts

Once you have written and produced your tract, the vital part comes next – using it! Carry copies with you in a back pocket, diary, handbag or the like. Every day, make sure you take some with you.

Give them to anyone you can (e.g. workmates, fellow students, parents you talk to at the school gate, people at the garage, supermarket, on the train/bus, as well as those on your Friendship List).

Key Scripture

KEY SCRIPTURE

Romans 10:9
"That if you confess with your mouth,
'Jesus is Lord,' and believe in your heart that God raised
him from the dead, you will be saved."

Session 5

A Spirit-filled Lifestyle

Welcome to Session Five of Blowing Your Cover. By now you should have benefited a great deal from the material already covered. You should be building relationships with non-Christians, praying for three names on your Friendship List and writing your personal tract. You now know how to share the gospel and, when appropriate, you are able to lead someone to Christ. However, without the work and influence of the Holy Spirit, you will be powerless and ineffective. Remember, evangelism is not just about learning a set of techniques, but allowing the Holy Spirit to empower your life through the fruit and gifts he develops within us.

If this is the case, obvious questions arise such as: Who is the Holy Spirit? How does he work in those who are unsaved and how does he want to work through you? These questions are covered in the aims below.

AIMS

1. To understand the role the Holy Spirit plays in evangelism
2. To look at the signs that follow your life
3. To pray for your friends

Key Scripture from Session Four

The Holy Spirit

Acts 1:8

"But you will receive power when the Holy Spirit comes on you; and you will be my witnesses in Jerusalem, and in all Judea and Samaria, and to the ends of the earth."

Who is the Holy Spirit?

The Holy Spirit is:

- The third person of the Trinity
- Fully God
- Eternal
- Omniscient
- Omnipresent
- He has a will
- He can speak

In evangelism the Holy Spirit works in two types of people:

- The unsaved
- The saved

Revelation 7:10
"Salvation belongs to our God..."

The whole of the conversion process is full of the activity of the Holy Spirit. He not only works in the messenger as he fills the believer with power, but also is powerfully at work in the life of the hearer (your friends) to whom he brings conviction of sin and, to others, conversion. Truly, salvation belongs to the Lord!

The Holy Spirit and your friends

As you pray and interact with those on your Friendship List and others that God brings across your path, the Holy Spirit works in two main ways.

Firstly, he starts to convict people of their sin. The Holy Spirit not only makes people aware of what is right and wrong but also makes people aware of a coming day of judgement, a time when lives will be evaluated and judged by the living God.

Secondly, the Holy Spirit continues to be actively involved in the lives of some of our non-Christian friends. Out of God's great mercy, the Holy Spirit continues to make people aware of their need for forgiveness and reconciliation. What's more, the Holy Spirit reveals to people that this was all made possible when Christ died on the cross in their place. This continued work of the Holy Spirit eventually leads to their conversion.

The Holy Spirit and conviction

Look at John 16:7–8. What is your responsibility in evangelism and what does the Holy Spirit do?

The Holy Spirit and conversion

Read Acts 8:26–39. How did the Holy Spirit guide Philip to Gaza? What do we learn about the way the Holy Spirit guides us as we seek to witness to others?

The Holy Spirit and you

The Holy Spirit not only works in the lives of our unsaved friends, but he also wants to work powerfully in your life as well. Lifestyle evangelism involves displaying the "fruit of the Spirit" as well as using the "gifts of the Spirit".

> ## Galatians 5:22–23
> "But the fruit of the Spirit is love, joy, peace, patience, kindness, goodness, faithfulness, gentleness and self-control."

As you live your life out in front of your family and friends they should see a difference in your lifestyle. The way we live influences others for better or worse regarding the gospel. When people look at your life what do they see?

Every believer has "signs" that follow their lives. They may be good signs or they may be bad signs. Scripture says that the fruit of the Spirit should be seen in a believer's life. Notice that the first fruit of the Spirit is love. Living a life displaying the fruit of the Spirit coupled with actively sharing the gospel can have a huge impact on those around you.

Evangelism is not just about what you do and say but also about who you are! As soon as you become a Christian, people begin to observe the way you live. Suddenly everything you do and how you do it becomes very public. Your whole life becomes evangelism; that is why the apostle Paul states that Christians are viewed as "living letters".

Many of your non-Christian friends as well as others in your sphere of influence have been watching how you live and act. Some are intrigued and may want to ask questions.

As well as the fruit of the Spirit let's look at the scripture verses below.

> ## 1 Thessalonians 1:4–5
> "For we know, brothers loved by God, that he has chosen you, because our gospel came to you not simply with words, but also with power, with the Holy Spirit and with deep conviction."

Notice that this is also the way Jesus wants us to evangelise. Jesus gave his disciples what they most needed, namely his power and authority. The Father gave his Son Jesus this power and authority and then Jesus gave this same power and authority to his disciples. So, what is power and authority?

- Power (Greek: *dunamis*) = the ability to do
- Authority (Greek: *exousia*) = the right to do

Jesus gives his disciples (you and me) the power of the Holy Spirit to get the job done, as well as his authority to exercise this power.

Having given his disciples power and authority, Jesus then gives his followers specific instructions in how they are to evangelise.

> ### Matthew 10:7
> **"As you go, preach this message:
> 'The kingdom of heaven is near.' Heal the sick..."**

Notice the phrase, **"As you go"**. These are the same words used in Matthew 28:18–20 as we read earlier in Session One.

Jesus spent a large proportion of his time bringing truth to people and healing the sick. How do you feel about engaging in such activities?

> ### Acts 1:8
> **"But you will receive power when the Holy Spirit comes on
> you; and you will be my witnesses in Jerusalem, and in all Judea
> and Samaria, and to the ends of the earth."**

This brings a personal challenge: How full of the Holy Spirit are you?

This statement has been described as the key to the book of Acts. After the day of Pentecost, a timid bunch of deserters were transformed into a dynamic company who marched all around the Mediterranean planting churches in one city after another.

- What transformed them?
- Where did they get such boldness to speak out about Christ?

Answer: They were **full** of the Holy Spirit.

If we want to fulfil God's plan for our lives and demonstrate the same boldness in our witness to others, then we must experience the Holy Spirit working through our lives, just as the disciples did.

Make a note of the different phrases used to describe this experience in the following verses.

Acts 1:5

Acts 1:8

Acts 2:4

Acts 2:17–21

Acts 2:38

Acts 10:44–45

Acts 11:15

**The Bible is very clear.
In order to live a Spirit-filled lifestyle you need
the Holy Spirit working in your life every day.**

Before we pray for each other, let's all pray together for two things: firstly, for our friends and, secondly, for the other members of your small-group.

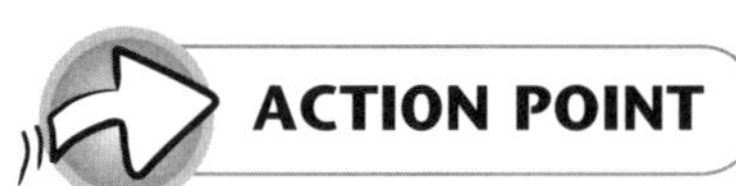

ACTION POINT

1. Let us pray for our friends

Pray for the three people on your Friendship List:

- That God will reveal himself more and that they will be open to his prompting

- That they will see how much better life can be with Christ than without him

- That they will see their need for his forgiveness

- That they will start to understand what Christ did on the cross and its relevance to them

- That they will attend a future Alpha or a similar enquirers' course

2. Now let us pray for your small group

Ask God to:

- Help us work together towards leading people to Jesus

- Help us encourage and support each other as we reach out to our friends

- Give wisdom to the group leaders as they seek to guide and advise us

- Give us many encouraging stories in the coming days ahead

3. Now let us pray for each other

Ask God to:

- Give you an anointing for the task

- Help you display the fruit of the Spirit as well as the gifts of the Spirit

- Use you to lead one person to Christ

- Make you open and honest in front of your friends

- Help you live a life consistent with the gospel

KEY SCRIPTURE

Romans 10:13
"Everyone who calls on the name of the Lord will be saved."

Session 6

Blowing Your Cover

Welcome to Session Six of Blowing Your Cover. In this session you will put into practice all you have learnt so far. It is time to consistently "blow your cover" and to enjoy being released into your lifestyle of evangelism. Imagine the impact on those in your village/town/city if everyone in your church were to embrace this challenge.

The aims for this session are stated below:

AIMS

1. To begin to put into practice what you have learnt so far
2. To enjoy spending time with your friends
3. To overcome fear
4. To blow your cover

Key Scripture from Session Five

Enjoying your lifestyle of evangelism

> ### John 10:10
> "The thief comes only to steal and kill and destroy;
> I have come that they *(God's children)* may have life
> and have it to the full."

This session is all about spending time with the friends on your Friendship List. The focus is not only on inviting these people along to relevant church meetings, but also about going out and spending time with them. Remember that throughout the course we have been provoked by the biblical emphasis of "as you go".

The challenge is to introduce other members of your church to your non-Christian friends. This is a BIG mindset change. Let me say it again. The challenge is to introduce other members of your church to your non-Christian friends… not the other way round. Obviously, think carefully about who you will introduce them to.

Your choice may be based on similar interests, or complementary evangelism styles, but whoever you choose, they need to be someone you know your non-Christian friends will enjoy meeting.

Here is a list of suggested activities that you could choose from (feel free to be inventive):

- Having a coffee with your friend/s
- Going tenpin bowling
- Doing some aspect of DIY together
- Going shopping with a friend
- Taking your friend and someone else from your group to the local pub's quiz night, or going out for the evening together
- Going to the local park with your friend, your child and their child
- Attending a concert or a sporting event together
- Going to the cinema
- Inviting a friend or neighbour to your house for a meal
- Doing a regular sporting or games activity
- Going for a walk in the countryside
- Taking part in a special interest activity (e.g. surfing, riding, photography)

In the space below, list two activities that you and your friends enjoy doing.

1.

2.

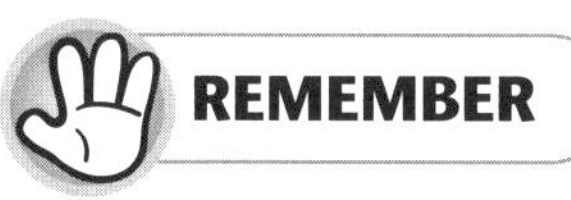

You may already be doing some of the things suggested here and developing friendships is a two-way street; be prepared for your friends to invite you out as well!

> **Luke 8:16**
> "No one lights a lamp and hides it in a jar or puts it under a bed. Instead, he puts it on a stand, so that those who come in can see the light."

The whole aim of Blowing Your Cover is to equip and release you to share your faith confidently and effectively. Having given consideration to what sort of activities you and your friends enjoy, we now want to focus on certain factors that can prevent you from meeting together. Some of these issues are simple practical matters; for instance, organising the time and place to meet one of the people on your Friendship List for a cup of coffee. Hopefully, these issues are easily dealt with; however, there are harder issues for some people.

Excuses, excuses and excuses...

What sort of things would stop you from inviting a friend to attend the next Alpha or similar enquirers' course?

In the boxes below write down as many excuses as you can think of:

Big excuse: FEAR

What is fear?

- **F**alse
- **E**xpectations
- **A**ppearing
- **R**eal

Someone once said that fear can come from our false expectations appearing real to each one of us. For instance, sometimes we don't bother asking people to meet us because our expectation is low. We automatically assume that people will say no when we ask them and often we don't bother to offer an invitation. This is wrong thinking. Because we are fishing in our "sphere of influence" (i.e. people we already have relationship with), just about everyone we ask may well respond positively to invitations. Be aware of wrong expectations.

> **"Let me assert my firm belief that the only thing
> we have to fear is fear itself."**
> (Franklin D. Roosevelt [1882–1945], US Democratic president.
> First Inaugural Address, 4 March 1933)

Fear can make us feel inadequate. We can be paralysed by thoughts such as, "What would I say to someone?" or "I don't think I'm particularly good at communicating well with others; I get completely tongue-tied." You may be thinking, "What if they reject me or don't want to listen to what I have to say? I would feel such a failure."

Be encouraged, Jeremiah had to deal with the same issues:

> **Jeremiah 1:6**
> **"Ah, Sovereign LORD," I said,**
> **"I do not know how to speak; I am only a child."**

How did God respond to Jeremiah? See Jeremiah 1:7–10:

The most important thing to remember as you engage in doing things that do not come easily is to know that **God is with you**. He is the one who helps you overcome timidity and fear. Your only requirement is to trust God. As you yield to God's control, he provides the opportunity, the power and the words. And even if one or two of your friends say, "Sorry, I can't come this time", you have nothing to feel bad about. It is normal… it's OK! No one can realistically attend everything. Taking this approach helps you to avoid disappointment.

> **2 Timothy 1:7–8**
> "For God did not give us a spirit of timidity, but a spirit of power, of love and of self-discipline. So do not be ashamed to testify about our Lord…"

Read Acts 4:1–15 and from these verses write down what you learn about the boldness of Peter and John before the Sanhedrin.

God wants you to be bold. He also wants you to believe that several of your friends will gladly enjoy your company and in time attend an Alpha or similar enquirers' course. Like Peter and John, we need to know that this boldness comes from being filled with the Holy Spirit. You need to be filled daily with the Holy Spirit and be ready to stand up and be counted.

> **Ezekiel 22:30**
>
> "I looked for a man among them who would build up
> the wall and stand before me in the gap."

Your checklist

You will be encouraged to meet up with your friends on a regular basis, and to spend quality time praying for them. Remember, these times should not add additional pressure to your life, but be something that you do naturally. In your small-group meetings you should pray for all the combined names on the group's Friendship List.

Finally, to help you monitor your progress and to apply everything you have learnt, a checklist is included.

It will expose areas in your life where you need help in evangelism. Remember, other members of your church have complementary styles that will help you in your witness to others. You are not meant to fish for people on your own. We are encouraged to fish together. We need each other. Biblical "fishing for people" is a community activity, not "one man and his rod"! Jesus always sent people out in pairs. He sent his disciples out in pairs for all sorts of tasks – to participate in village evangelism, to secure the use of a room for the Passover meal and even to collect a donkey for him to ride on into Jerusalem!

Biblical evangelism means working mainly as a team, not on your own.

The checklist

The following checklist will help you monitor your progress. When reviewing these questions tick the line for encouragement and let the unticked lines bring the challenge.

_____ Do you know the main evangelism "style" of at least three other friends in your church?

_____ Are you aware of two others whose "style" complements your "style" of evangelism?

_____ Are you praying regularly for the three people on your Friendship List?

_____ Have you recently enjoyed spending time with any of the three names on your Friendship List – for instance, lunch, coffee or a chance meeting?

_____ Are you learning to listen actively to your friends?

_____ Have you had a good conversation with any of these three people recently?

_____ Did you turn any of these conversations towards biblical truths?

_____ Have you had an opportunity in the last month to pass on your story to any of your non-Christian friends?

_____ Have you introduced any of your church friends to the people on your Friendship List?

_____ Have you finished writing up your personal tract?

_____ Have you had your personal tract printed (e.g. using a computer)?

_____ Have you given a copy of your personal tract to a non-Christian since you last reviewed this checklist?

_____ Have you shared the "picture gospel outline" with anyone on your Friendship List?

_____ Have you prayed WITH any of your friends recently?

_____ Have you ever invited any of the above to an Alpha or similar enquirers' course?

_____ Have you been that all-important "link in the chain"?

_____ Have you seen anyone on your Friendship List become a Christian?

What happens next?

There is always a real sense of excitement when someone has become a Christian and been added to the church. There are even greater celebrations when whole families are saved!

Through participating in Blowing Your Cover you have identified your unique evangelism style and learnt that you can actually enjoy evangelism! You have been shown the principles of effective communication of the gospel and practised telling your personal story and leading someone to Christ. You have been empowered with the Holy Spirit and are now ready to see people saved and added to your local church.

So now it is time for the "rubber to hit the road"! Be bold, be confident, live your life out of the knowledge of who you are in Christ. Finally and most importantly, be who God intended you to be... *yourself.*

> **Matthew 28:18 20**
> **Then Jesus came to them and said, "All authority in heaven and on earth has been given to me. Therefore go and make disciples of all nations, baptising them in the name of the Father and of the Son and of the Holy Spirit, and teaching them to obey everything I have commanded you. And surely I am with you always, to the very end of the age."**

THE END?

Only the beginning...

Appendix
A Cultural Overview of Western Society

Starting notes

- In Western culture "modern" refers to a period of time, not to the idea of being "technologically up to date".

- In the Workbook we have only written a short paragraph about different cultures. These extra notes will help you understand the concepts of "pre-modern", "modern" and "post-modern" cultures. Disbelievers, Doubters, Observers and Seekers on your Friendship Lists are profoundly influenced by culture. Through these additional notes you will be able to discover how the Western worldview has developed, where you fit into this worldview and also where your friends fit into it.

- Further reading:

  ○ Nick Pollard, *Evangelism Made Slightly Less Difficult*, IVP

  ○ Michael Green, *Critical Choices*, Hodder & Stoughton

  ○ Nick Spencer, *Beyond Belief*, LICC Publications

  ○ Mark Greene, *Imagine* DVD, LICC Publications, UK only

  ○ All resources can be purchased through our online store: www.blowingyourcover.com

- The six Blowing Your Cover principles relating to culture outlined in these notes are:

  ○ Principle One: Pre-modern thought

  ○ Principle Two: Modern thought

  ○ Principle Three: Post-modern thought

  ○ Principle Four: Western worldview

  ○ Principle Five: Christian worldview

  ○ Principle Six: Imposition?

Principle One: **Pre-modern thought**

In "pre-modern times" (up to about 1600) people viewed humanity and the world around them as God's creation. When they wanted to discover the truth, they turned to the church. There was a strong belief in sacred texts, such as the Bible, and a strong community life. However, as many people were illiterate this led to "prescribed thought".

Pre-modern viewpoints

Small narrative

A narrative is a worldview, the picture that people have of their world. In pre-modern times this was a small, local viewpoint. People did not travel far and everything they needed was provided in the village area.

Providence

Providence was almost fatalistic and lay in the hands of God. Due to the level of illiteracy, people's view of providence was governed by what they heard from the church. Providence was therefore seen as God's will being applied to daily life.

One truth

The worldview at the time was small, therefore the only accepted truth was the one supplied by the church. There was very little influence from other religions and therefore what was relevant to one person was consequently relevant to the whole village.

Pre-critical

Within this era people did not question beliefs, motives or authority. Many things were taken for granted without being thought through.

Representative building

A building that would typify this period would be Cologne Cathedral. Work began in 1247 and took over 600 years to complete. It was built for the glory of God, points to heaven and was used for worship.

Principle Two: **Modern thought**

In "modern" times (1600–1960) people's views started to change, primarily because of the French Renaissance and the influence of Descartes whose main work was published in 1637. He is described as the father of modern thought and coined the phrase, "I think therefore I am". Society was characterised by reason and rationality (what can be proved to be certain). This resulted in a subtle shift to throw out sacred texts and inhibit the display of emotions (e.g. in the Victorian period this led to the British "stiff upper lip"). Science declared that it would provide all the answers by proof and certainty. This period of time was described as "The Enlightenment". During this period, with the advent of the printing press, people became increasingly more literate.

Modern viewpoints

Meta-narrative

In the modern era a "bigger picture" worldview has increasingly developed. As travel increases, so people's concepts and beliefs are challenged. People are aware of other faiths but remain faithful to their heritage.

Cause and effect

With the advance of science, people begin to question the simple ideas of providence. They push the boundaries and discover cause and effect. This makes a huge impact on society. Darwin's theory of evolution promotes cause and effect, which subtly erodes the meta-narrative of Christianity in society.

Method

Truth in a modern society can only be accepted if it can be proved. Science refines new ideas and subsequently declares that it can provide answers to life's questions, even the deepest questions of life. However, the thought that science can save the world is hopelessly optimistic.

Critical

In this era people begin to analyse things more and more and to question authority and traditional belief systems.

However, this era did not produce the harmony that the modern prophets predicted. After two world wars, slavery, communism, Nazism and two nuclear bombs, people began to question whether reason, technology and science could make a better world. In the 21st century the influence of modernism has not ended, though we are in its last days. As modernism falls, so post-modernism rises to take its place.

Representative building

A building that would characterise this period would be the Eiffel Tower. It was built in 1889 and until 1930 was the world's tallest building. It was celebrated as one of modern man's great achievements.

Principle Three: **Post-modern thought**

"Post-modernism" started in the 1960s. Philosophers are not agreed on what to call the period we now live in. Some have suggested the "post post-modern" period. However, when people look back they may well entitle this period "The Disillusionment". Never have so many people been so unhappy and desired something better. In post-modern culture it is easier to proclaim the gospel. With the decline of reason our Christian view is just as relevant as any other religious viewpoint. However, how we initially present it is of great importance. If we strongly assert "the truth" too soon, we are seen as narrow-minded. Post-modern thinking says there is no one truth. An interesting point to note is that other major religions make similar claims.

Post-modern viewpoints

Episodes
In a post-modern world, the meta-narrative is replaced with episodes. This can be seen predominantly through the media. Once, programmes followed a single theme throughout the broadcast; now each programme is broken down into smaller, more manageable portions. We have become a sound-bite generation.

Chance and mystery
Cause and effect have been replaced to a large extent by chance. People have a more fatalistic approach to life. There has been a huge increase in the rise of mysticism (e.g. belief in horoscopes, spiritualism, etc.).

Choice and pleasure
In a post-modern society there is a "pick and mix" approach to life. Post-modern thought states that to choose is to live, and that having no choice is fatal. We are encouraged to live for today and have fun.

However, in post-modernism there are no absolutes. If you want to know what is true then you consult your feelings and make your personal choice.

Representative building
A building that embodies this period is the Millennium Dome. It was built in 1999 and encompassed many different and sometimes contradictory messages. Within a year of its closure it lay empty, unused and semi-derelict!

Principle Four: **Western worldview**

Below are some answers to the above questions. Note that not all of Western society's values are negative ones.

Western viewpoints

Reason/rationality
Men and women are able to find the facts/answers to everything.

Experiences
In Western thinking, experiences are vitally important. Whether good or bad, they shape each one of us.

Traditions and superstitions
Halloween, Christmas and Mother's Day play a central part in our culture.

Environment
We are constantly barraged with the problems and potential problems of the environment.

Sex
This is a boom industry in Western culture and invades our lives through the influence of the media.

Money
This drives Western economies. If the stock markets were to collapse what would happen?

Leisure
This is another massive industry. People want more leisure time because they work longer hours. People live for the weekends and their next holiday.

Family upbringing
This affects the way we think and live. We are becoming increasingly individualistic. Yet secretly people long to belong to something.

Spirituality
New Age, Islam and horoscopes play a huge part in Western culture. People are looking for answers in some sort of spirituality. This leads to a problem with the uniqueness of Jesus and Christianity. A belief in one exclusive way to God is not a popular cultural message.

Principle Five: Christian worldview

Compare Western and Christian worldviews. Paul says in Romans 12:2, "Do not conform any longer to the pattern of this world, but be transformed by the renewing of your mind."

Christian viewpoints

Jesus-centred
All answers are found in Jesus. He is the Son of God.

The Holy Bible
The Bible is absolute truth and therefore is relevant to every generation.

The Church
The Church represents Christ to the world. The local church is the hope for the world.

Faith
This is the opposite of cynicism. How many of us are cynical about our faith?

Vision
God has a plan and a purpose for each one of us.

Humility

This is the opposite of pride.

Service

This is the opposite of status. Loyalty and servanthood are not high values in Western thinking.

Compassion

This is the opposite of selfishness.

Purity/holiness

Living to please God is a completely different outlook on life from that expressed by today's society.

Generosity

This is the opposite of selfishness.

Principle Six: Imposition?

ASK YOURSELF

As you connect with your culture and build relationships with those in your sphere of influence, can you impose your viewpoint on others?

In a post-modern world how can you present the gospel, demonstrate your faith and give people an opportunity to know more about Jesus?

Bibliography

We would like to acknowledge and recommend the following resources. They have helped shape our thinking and will provide further stimulus to any reader.

Aldrich, Joseph C.; *Lifestyle Evangelism*, Multnomah Press, 1999

Allan, John; *Just Looking*, Bible Society, 1987

Bell, Arnold; *Postmodernism 1997 Stoneleigh Tape*, Newfrontiers,

Bruce, F.F.; *The Spreading Flame*, Paternoster Press, 1964

Chantry, Walter; *Today's Gospel: Authentic or Synthetic?*, Banner of Truth Trust, 1996

Coleman, Robert; *The Master Plan of Evangelism*, Revell, 1986

Drummond, Lewis A.; *The Evangelist: The Worldwide Impact of Billy Graham*, Word, 2001

Edwins, Dave; *Moorlands College Level 2 Evangelism Notes*, 2002

Ford, Kevin; *Jesus for a New Generation*, IVP, 1995

Frost, Rob; *Pilgrims*, Kingsway,

Green, Michael; *Evangelism Now and Then*, IVP, 1979

Green, Michael; *Critical Choices*, Hodder & Stoughton,

Gumbel, Nicky; *The Alpha Initiative*, Alpha Products,

Houston, Brian; *For This Cause*, Maximised Leadership Series, 2001

Hull, Bill; *The Disciple-Making Pastor*, Revell, 1999

Mahaney, C.J.; *Why Small Groups?*, PDI, 1996

Manley Pippert, Rebecca; *Out of the Salt Shaker*, IVP, 1999

Mittleberg, Strobel and Hybels; *Becoming a Contagious Christian*, Zondervan, 1996

Nouwen, Henri J.M.; *In The Name of Jesus*, Darton, Longman & Todd, 1989

Peterson, Jim; *Evangelism as a Lifestyle*, Navpress, 1980

Pollard, Nick; *Evangelism Made Slightly Less Difficult*, IVP, 1997

Singlehurst, Laurence; *Sowing Reaping Keeping*, Crossways Books,

Sjogren, Steve, *Irresistible Evangelism*, Group publishing, 2004

Snyder, Howard A. *et al*; *The Radical Wesley and Patterns for Church Renewal*, IVP, 1980

Sprenger, Mike; *Total Evangelism*, Newfrontiers,

Strobel, Lee; *Inside the Mind of Unchurched Harry and Mary*, Zondervan, 1993

Tomczak, Larry; *Divine Appointments*, Kingsway,

Virgo, Terry; *Weak People Mighty God*, Kingsway,

Wimber, John; *Power Evangelism*, Hodder & Stoughton, 2001

Wright, N.T.; *Jesus and the Victory of God*, SPCK, 1996

Yancey, Philip; *What's So Amazing about Grace?*, HarperCollins, 1997

Additional Notes

Additional Notes

Additional Notes

Additional Notes

Additional Notes

Additional Notes